101 Ways to Be a Special Mom

101 Ways to Be a Special Mom

VICKI LANSKY

Illustrations by Kaye Pomeranc White

CONTEMPORARY BOOKS

Library of Congress Cataloging-in-Publication Data

Lansky, Vicki.
    101 ways to be a special mom / Vicki Lansky.
        p.   cm.
    ISBN 0-8092-3530-7
    1. Mother and child—United States—Miscellanea.   2. Parenting—
United States—Miscellanea.   3. Child rearing—United States—Miscellanea.
I. Title.   II. Title: One hundred and one ways to be a special mom.
III. Title: Hundred and one ways to be a special mom.
HQ755.85L356   1995
649'.1—dc20   94-42593
                                                               CIP

Published by Contemporary Books
A division of NTC/Contemporary Publishing Group, Inc.
4255 West Touhy Avenue, Lincolnwood (Chicago), Illinois 60646-1975 U.S.A.
International Standard Book Number: 0-8092-3530-7

20   19   18   17   16   15   14   13   12   11

To
Mary Kaplan Rogosin,
1907–1991.
You were definitely a very special mom.
Lucky me. Thank you.

Acknowledgments

Thanks to the following people, whose ideas are included in this book: Dawna Brown of Ontario, Canada; Denise Davis of Indianapolis; Pam Jarmon of Houston; Joy Knudson of Everett, Washington; Mary Louise Kutsch of Ridgeway, Pennsylvania; Eileen Pankow of Lithonia, Georgia; Connie Peter of Lockhart, Texas; and Debbie Skinner of Elm City, North Carolina.

Introduction

The most treasured memories of childhood are often of those small acts of kindness and tenderness, the things the loving adults in our life did for us. We carry these with us forever. They become emotional savings that we can fall back on when necessary. They give us riches beyond gold and compensation for many of life's harsher moments.

Many of our loving efforts for our children are made automatically. Often in the busyness of life, however, we have to work at creating special moments, and sometimes our inspiration runs dry. You are not expected to put each of the ideas in this book into action. Instead, read through for ideas that fit your parenting style. Some may become new family traditions, or you may find yourself saying "Oh, I'd love to do that" or "Why didn't I do that the other night?" When you read through this book again in a year or two, other ideas might be more timely or doable than they are now.

You'll find other suggestions in my books

101 Ways to Be a Special Dad, 101 Ways to Make Your Child Feel Special, and *101 Ways to Tell Your Child "I Love You."* I've tried not to repeat here the ideas offered in those earlier books, though you may find a few that are. Or you might already use ideas that are not here but are in my other books. No doubt you have traditions that I haven't even listed.

Finally, don't wait for time tomorrow to make room for special moments and memories. Too often we don't do things today if we feel we can make time tomorrow. Yet our children's lives soon become as complicated and harried as ours, and you will find that tomorrow has suddenly become yesterday. Take advantage of the days when your children are sweet and young, for your sake as well as theirs.

101 Ways to Be a Special Mom

Kiss all owies!

Wear a T-shirt
with your child's name on it.

When you wake your child in the morning, bring a cup of juice. A short back rub and, if time permits, reading a story make a great way to start the day!

Plan a winter camp-out, or rather a camp-in. Bring out the sleeping bags and set up your campsite in the living room (no TV, please). Use flashlights, tell stories, eat popcorn, and, if you have a fireplace, roast hot dogs or toast marshmallows for S'mores.

Make hot chocolate—and don't forget to add a few mini-marshmallows!

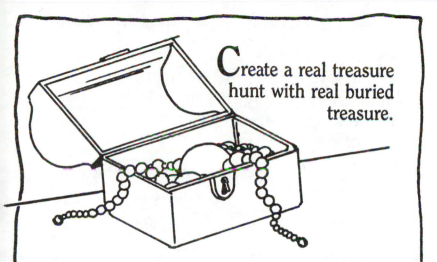

Create a real treasure hunt with real buried treasure.

Bury a box filled with old costume jewelry (check out garage sale finds) in the yard or garden. Write and hide clues leading ultimately to a treasure map with the appropriate X noted. Mark the spot with an X so they dig in the right place.

Promise to double whatever money your children save during the three to five months before their birthday or a holiday.

Keep various cookie cutters or clean scissors handy to make food fun!

Cut designs out of cheese slices,
cold cuts,
sandwiches,
even Jell-O.

Once a year (birthdays are the easiest to remember), trace an outline of your child on a paintable wall. Make a new outline each year, indicating the date and the child's age. Photograph it for posterity if you move or have to paint the wall.

Lauren
1995
7 yrs.

Michael
1995
5 yrs.

Build in an extra half hour when doing errands to allow for a stop at any park you pass. Try to find parks with adult-size swings as well as smaller ones for your child so you can be a participant rather than a spectator. A memorable time out!

Let your child pick your lottery numbers.

You just might get lucky!

I'm Sorry, Sweetheart.

Apologize to your child when you say something you regret. Not being afraid to admit that even moms make mistakes is a way of showing respect and love for your child.

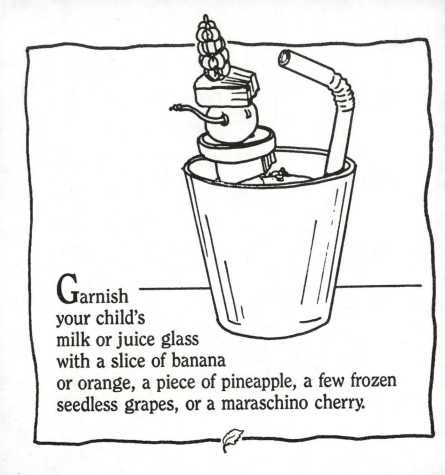

Garnish
your child's
milk or juice glass
with a slice of banana
or orange, a piece of pineapple, a few frozen
seedless grapes, or a maraschino cherry.

Write a message on the napkin you put in your child's lunch box.

Or perk up a brown bag by drawing a picture on it.

Agree to a particular time when you'll send each other "love vibrations" when you won't be together.

Later, talk about how special you felt knowing your child was thinking of you.

Hors d'oeuvre platters are a nice variation on the milk and cookies routine for a child just home from school. Even if you won't be there yourself, an hors d'oeuvre plate (with a nice love note attached) greeting a child who always heads for the refrigerator first will be remembered warmly. Try little vegetables like baby carrots and cherry tomatoes, cubes of cheese, dip, and breadsticks.

Leave a project for your child and sitter when you'll be out for an evening. Have all the materials ready. Modeling dough, clay, paints, or beadwork can be fun even for a sitter and lessens reliance on TV as entertainment.

How about a simple cooking project? Leave cookie dough in the refrigerator along with sprinkles, raisins, little candies, and icing for decorating.

Stay at the bus stop waving and throwing kisses until the bus is out of view, especially for the first day of school or for a birthday. If your schedule allows, do it daily! Be sure to stop when your child clues you that he or she is too old for this special treatment.

Create a special treasure box for yourself to keep items your child gives to you.

Make a weekly date with your child, if your schedule allows. Let your child pick the activity—within appropriate limits. Younger children will do better choosing from several possibilities offered by you—and you won't risk spoiling the fun by having to reject their suggestions.

Date with Addie on Monday

Have dinner by candlelight. Let your child choose a favorite meal for that evening.

For a special outing together, take one child to a movie without other siblings or adults. Impromptu weekend lunches are another way of doing this.

Take time to rock an older child, at bedtime, just for time to talk together, or for some needed quiet time. If your child feels *too* old for this, you'll hear about it.

Commandeer a large appliance box when the opportunity arises. It should be big enough to be turned into a fort, a lemonade stand, a puppet show theater, a spaceship, or a house. Provide markers, scraps of fabric, leftover wallpaper, and other items for decorating.

CLUB HOUSE

MAIL

Help with the necessary cutting out of doors and windows.

Select a bird feeder together and assign your child the job of keeping it stocked. Maybe even name it for your child (e.g., Sara's Seed Salon, Eric's Sunflower Solarium). Spend time together discussing or drawing its visitors, perhaps identifying them with the help of a local field guide.

Use a flashlight to point to things in the dark when putting a child to bed. Doing this can demonstrate that things that look scary in the dark are really harmless. Give the child a flashlight too and take turns shining the beam on the same or different objects. Leave the flashlight with your bedtime bambino as a "security blanket."

Purchase cheap props at garage sales for a dress-up box. Donate some of your old hats, gloves, shoes, and clothes to that box, too.

Have you ever gone to a U-pick-it farm?

They can be found everywhere and make for a wonderful outing. You'll find strawberries, raspberries, blueberries, corn, beans, and cucumbers. Most important, make at least one trip to a pumpkin patch!

Let your children
hear stories of
your childhood.

They love knowing
that you were
little once, just
like them.

At the first sign of spring, buy a container of bubble-blowing mix to play with outside as part of a recognized seasonal rite. (If you're an adventurous mom, these can be played with inside your car too before you get home from the store.)

Do your best to show up for school events and performances. Children may never remember when you come, but they'll never forget when you don't.

Be willing to have your child's team organizational meeting or school newspaper layout project on your turf. It is worth the necessary extra cleanup time.

After wrapping your child in a towel following a bath or shower, add a towel hug as part of the drying process.

Instead of a back rub, make stroking your child's forehead part of your bedtime routine. Or save this as a technique to use just when your child is ill or unhappy.

Occasionally taking time out together to lie on a bed or on the floor while listening to your favorite classical music or relaxation tape can be very enjoyable.

Tuck your child in with a blanket
wherever they fall asleep, be it
a chair,
a couch,
the car,
or her
own bed.

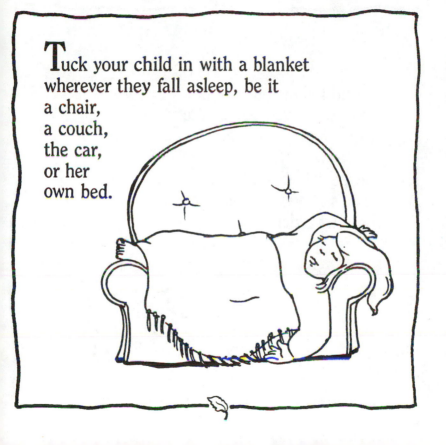

Hold hands when going for a walk even when safety is no longer a concern.

(Respect your children's wishes about this as they get older.)

Let your child turn the pages of the book or magazine you are reading together. When he's old enough, let him read each chapter title or especially funny bits of dialogue.

If you like to jog, let your child bike along with you.

Take your children to the mailbox or post office to mail their letters to Santa.

Get season tickets to something—anything that your budget allows—to assure that you'll make time for a certain number of enriching outings. It gives everyone something to look forward to. Or encourage this as an activity to be done with nearby grandparents.

Learn to say
"I'm sorry that didn't work out"
or
"The same thing happened to me once,"
or
"I know that's hard on you"

(rather than "I told you so").

Always give your children hello and good-bye kisses.

Display your children's artwork—as well as photographs of them—in conspicuous places. Attractive cardboard picture frames make it easy to change them.

Keep your child up-to-date on family and extended family news. This way family closeness can develop even when relatives are many miles away.

We both love it!

Cover for a child—occasionally—who forgets to say thank you in a timely fashion by saying

"Thank you from both of us."

Constantly correcting children in front of others doesn't always teach the lesson you want them to learn.

Join your children in sandbox play.

Talk to your children about your job or volunteer work outside the home in concrete details. Take them along on occasion and let them take something to keep to make them feel a part of your life away from them.

Buy pre-made pizza crust, sauce, cheese, and toppings and let your child be in charge of making a fun and special meal for everyone.

Take advantage of chauffeuring time for a good chat or even small talk. (Discourage radio use unless you're on a long trip, everyone is singing along, or it's been a really bad day.)

Don't let your child's childhood pass without teaching and playing games unique to our culture: old maid, bingo, war, concentration, go fish, Uno, Scrabble, Monopoly, checkers, tic-tac-toe, dot-to-dot, etc.

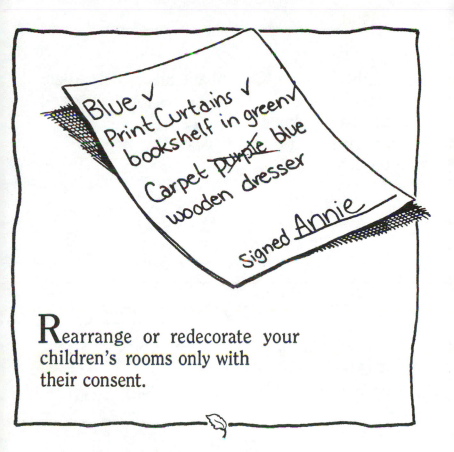

Rearrange or redecorate your children's rooms only with their consent.

When your children get older, help them make their own appointments for doctor and dentist checkups, haircuts, and the like.

Then give them full responsibility. It's your job to lose parts of your job as they mature.

Rake fall leaves with the understanding that a pile of leaves must be jumped on before being bagged.

Take a coffee break together.

Heat up milk in a mug for your child, pour in a spoonful or two of coffee, offer some sweetener, stir, and sit down for a time-out together.

Save the fortune cookie you picked up at lunch or the night before for your child to open and share with you.

Repeat—over time—the story of each child's birth. Kids love hearing about the day they were born. Make this a yearly tradition by doing this on each child's birthday.

Create a song, poem, or story using your child's name.

Mia is my sweet, sweet pea. She's the best thing that ever happened to me. I love her more than I can tell. She's funny, sweet and oh so swell!!

Leave love notes before you go off on a business (or pleasure) trip and send mail while away.

Call, too!

When dealing with behavior problems, ask your child for input regarding punishment or motivating a behavior change. You might be surprised by what your child comes up with.

Make a
rainy day special.

Get out your umbrellas and raincoats and
enjoy a warm, wet walk. Or climb under the
covers for a snuggle, cuddle, or nap together.

Make the entire day special for your child's birthday. This doesn't have to be elaborate or costly, and the focus doesn't have to be on parties and gift giving. A special day of one's own is the best gift you can give a child.

Surprise your child with a birthday banner or other decorations that he or she will see upon waking, and then serve a mini-bagel or muffin with a candle in it for breakfast. Carry on throughout the day, perhaps bringing it to a close with a favorite bedtime story—plus an extra to grow on!

Read to your children.

Read stories at bedtime, read under the covers with a flashlight, read parts of the newspaper during breakfast, and read to your kids even after they are able to read by themselves. It may or may not turn your child into a book reader, but reading together will create warm feelings of closeness that are worth every moment.

Begin a family diary.

Use a school notebook that each member writes in (even if just at bedtime) or dictates thoughts to you. You don't need to make entries every day—maybe just every Friday night. Be sure to include special annual events such as the first day of school, birthdays, and the first bike ride without training wheels.

As you do chores or activities together, take a moment to deliver a kiss to the top of that terrific little head.

If you don't have time to watch a whole videotape together, do it in ten- to fifteen-minute intervals (as though you were reading a chapter of a book) with the understanding that this is ". . . to be continued."

Create a floral arrangement using your child as your helper.

Don't just stick bought or picked flowers into a vase. Place them there one at a time, deciding where to cut the stem, removing lower leaves, and creating an attractive and thought-out arrangement.

Catch your child at being good . . .
and then be generous
with compliments.

Let your child be the surprise dinner guest.

Explain that someone special
is coming for dinner.
Clean up the house.
Set the table with
your good dishes.
At dinnertime, pin a
flower on your child
and explain that your
child is your
        special dinner guest!

Always have one camera on hand
with film in it to capture the
fun of unexpected events
you'll want to remember.

Teach your child
your particular
skills (crocheting,
cooking, golf,
painting,
and so on)
just for the fun—not the perfection—of it.

S et up a family bulletin board.

As well as memos, to-do lists, and photos of relatives, post notices of your child's accomplishments.

When you're babyproofing your home, take extra measures to create an environment where you don't have to say no more than necessary.

Don't think only of safety but of the joy of free exploration.

Huddle together during thunderstorms.
It's not necessary
for anyone to   brave it alone.

Occasional
fun fights—
with pillows or
squirt guns—are
long remembered.

When leaving kids
for an out-of-town trip,
leave small wrapped gifts to
be opened each day at a given time
while you're away.

Keep a family travel journal documenting each special trip you take. Make daily entries of your activities, including your child's impressions and funny or otherwise interesting happenings. Tuck this away with photos from your trips, and you'll be able to relive details for years to come.

Our Trip to Williamsburg 1995

Skip down your street, driveway, or sidewalk—or even at the mall—with your children to their delight.

Encourage—and enjoy—moments of being goofy or silly.

That's right! She got all "A"s

One way to emphasize a compliment is to make a pretend call to a newspaper, TV or radio station, national magazine, or even the White House to give your report. Tell your child, "That's incredible. I've just got to call —— and tell them about this." Then dial a partial number and "report the news" over the phone.

Invest in a subscription to a child's magazine. Not only will it bring your child mail over the course of the year, but it will give you something else to read together.

Carry up-to-date photos of your children in your wallet. Check that their dad has current ones also.

Reinforce your children's relationships with their grandparents and extended family. You can do this by encouraging them to make phone calls and send thank-you notes and by suggesting activities they can do together.

For a special occasion
or to make a depressing day end on an up
note, prepare or give a bath by candlelight.

Send a letter, package, or magazine to arrive before your children at summer camp so they have mail at the first mail call.

Leave the empty chocolate icing or whipped cream bowls and beaters for your kids to lick clean.

When they are small,
let your children experience with you at their
side those larger-than-life events—parades,
circuses, zoos, train rides, etc.—where they
will feel safe in your presence.

Remember that children usually need love most when they deserve it the least. What makes mothers so special is that they love their children even when things go wrong.

Periodically go through your jewelry box with your child.

Children long remember playing with pieces and hearing stories about special items. Let a child know what heirloom will be passed on to him or her.

Share or start a collection
with each child.

It will give you an interest to share and
something to shop together for, at or away
from home.

Celebrate a special feat or occasion by greeting your little celebrity with one or more helium balloons.

Keep art supplies easily accessible.

Just a box filled with crayons, markers, paper, glue, stencils, and other stuff for collages will inspire most children.

ART STUFF

When was the last time you looked deeply into your child's eyes for at least five seconds? There is no better way to see—or be seen by—a child.

Make your home a comfortable place for your children to bring their friends.

It means extra juice and cookies, more art supplies, even more TV watched, but you'll know where your children are and how they are spending their time.

Keep the promises you make
and don't make promises
you can't keep.

Go through a cookbook with your child and decide on a new recipe that you will make together or create a new one  and call it,

for example: SOPHIE'S SNACKS

Never worry about
using an extra bandage
on an unseen owie.

Be sure to build in some hanging-out-together time on a regular basis. One of the best places for hanging out is sprawled on your big bed.

Make seasonal holidays special with some annual traditions—carving a pumpkin the week before Halloween, having an annual spring egg hunt, making a gingerbread house out of graham crackers iced to small milk cartons at Christmastime.

Limit yourself to a reasonable number of traditions that you and your kids can look forward to.

Don't be afraid to show your love
by simply saying no
when necesssary.

It's okay to be the brick wall your children
must push against to learn about limits.

Vicki Lansky has written more than twenty-five books in which she shares what has worked for her and others. For a free catalog of her other books, just drop a note to the address below or call 1-800-255-3379.

Vicki Lansky
c/o Practical Parenting™
Department M
Deephaven, MN 55391

If you enjoyed *101 Ways to Be a Special Mom*, you'll also appreciate Vicki Lansky's other Contemporary classics, *101 Ways to Tell Your Child "I Love You," 101 Ways to Make Your Child Feel Special*, and *101 Ways to Be a Special Dad*. They are available in your local bookstore.